MW01486842

First Biographies

Sam Houston

by Lisa Trumbauer

Consulting Editor: Gail Saunders-Smith, Ph.D.
Consultant: Richard B. Rice, M.A.
Historical Interpreter, Sam Houston Memorial Museum
Huntsville, Texas

Capstone
press

Mankato, Minnesota

Pebble Books are published by Capstone Press
151 Good Counsel Drive, P.O. Box 669, Mankato, Minnesota 56002
http://www.capstonepress.com

1 2 3 4 5 6 09 08 07 06 05 04

Library of Congress Cataloging-in-Publication Data
Trumbauer, Lisa, 1963–
Sam Houston / by Lisa Trumbauer.
    p. cm.—(First biographies)
    Summary: Simple text and photographs introduce the life of Sam Houston,
who served as governor of Texas after helping fight for the region's independence
from Mexico.
    Includes bibliographical references and index.
    ISBN 0-7368-2370-0 (hardcover)
    1. Houston, Sam, 1793–1863—Juvenile literature. 2. Governors—Texas—
Biography—Juvenile literature. 3. Legislators—United States—Biography—Juvenile
literature. 4. United States. Congress. Senate—Biography—Juvenile literature.
5. Texas—History—To 1846—Juvenile literature. [1. Houston, Sam, 1793–1863.
2. Governors. 3. Legislators. 4. Texas—History—To 1846.] I. Title. II. First
biographies (Mankato, Minn.)
F390.H84T78 2004
976.4'04'092—dc21   2003011424

Note to Parents and Teachers

The First Biographies series supports national history standards for
units on people and culture. This book describes and illustrates the
life of Sam Houston. The photographs support early readers in
understanding the text. This book also introduces early readers to
subject-specific vocabulary words, which are defined in the
Glossary. Early readers may need assistance to read some words
and to use the Table of Contents, Glossary, Read More, Internet
Sites, and Index/Word List sections of the book.

Table of Contents

BIRTHPLACE OF
SAM HOUSTON

ON MARCH 2, 1793, THE NOTED SOLDIER AND STATESMAN SAM
HOUSTON WAS BORN IN A LOG CABIN ON A NEARBY KNOLL.
HOUSTON SERVED WITH DISTINCTION IN THE U.S. ARMY AND
LATER AS A CONGRESSMAN AND GOVERNOR OF TENNESSEE
BEFORE MOVING TO TEXAS IN THE 1830s. IN TEXAS, HE SOON
BECAME A LEADER IN THE REVOLUTION AGAINST THE MEXICAN
GOVERNMENT UNDER GENERAL ANTONIO LOPEZ DE SANTA ANNA.
A SIGNER OF THE TEXAS DECLARATION OF INDEPENDENCE ON
MARCH 2, 1836, HOUSTON WAS CHOSEN COMMANDER-IN-CHIEF OF
THE TEXIAN ARMY. ON APRIL 21, 1836, HE LED HIS FORCES TO
VICTORY IN THE BATTLE OF SAN JACINTO, WHICH RESULTED
IN THE INDEPENDENCE OF TEXAS.

SAM HOUSTON TWICE SERVED AS PRESIDENT OF THE REPUBLIC
OF TEXAS. LATER, AFTER TEXAS BECAME PART OF THE UNITED
STATES OF AMERICA, HE SERVED AS U.S. SENATOR AND AS
GOVERNOR. HE DIED AT HIS HOME IN HUNTSVILLE, TEXAS, ON
JULY 26, 1863, DURING THE CIVIL WAR, A STRUGGLE HE
BITTERLY OPPOSED.

AN ABLE GENERAL, A STRONG POLITICAL LEADER, AND A FRIEND
TO THE CHEROKEE INDIANS WHO KNEW HIM AS "THE RAVEN," SAM
HOUSTON REPRESENTED THE TRUE SPIRIT OF HIS NATIVE
VIRGINIA AND HIS ADOPTED STATES OF TENNESSEE AND TEXAS.

Time Line

1793
born

1808
runs away
from home

Young Sam

Sam Houston was born in Virginia in 1793. He and his family moved to Tennessee in 1806. When Sam was 15, he ran away. He lived with the Cherokee Indians for three years.

marker showing the birthplace of Sam Houston

Time Line

1793
born

1808
runs away
from home

Sam loved to read. He
taught school for one year.
Sam was a good teacher
and storyteller. His students
enjoyed learning from him.

the schoolhouse where Sam taught

Time Line

1793
born

1808
runs away
from home

1814
fights in
U.S. Army

8

In 1813, Sam became a soldier. He was wounded in a battle. Sam was in the U.S. Army for five years.

a soldier pulls an arrow from Sam's leg during a battle

Time Line

1793
born

10

1808
runs away
from home

1814
fights in
U.S. Army

1823
elected to
Congress

A Life in Politics

In 1818, Sam began working as a lawyer. He was elected to Congress in 1823. In 1827, Sam became the governor of Tennessee.

Sam as a congressman in 1826

Time Line

1793	1808	1814	1823
born	runs away from home	fights in U.S. Army	elected to Congress

Sam quit as governor in 1829. He became a member of the Cherokee Nation. He owned a trading post. Sam was chosen to speak for Cherokee rights in Washington, D.C.

◄ the trading post that Sam owned;
Sam dressed in Cherokee clothing.

Time Line

1793
born

1808
runs away
from home

1814
fights in
U.S. Army

1823
elected to
Congress

In 1832, President Andrew Jackson asked Sam to work with American Indians in Texas. At that time, Texas was a part of Mexico. In 1836, Texas wanted to be free from Mexico.

Sam dressed in Cherokee clothing

1829
becomes
Cherokee member

Time Line

1793
born

1808
runs away
from home

1814
fights in
U.S. Army

1823
elected to
Congress

16

In 1836, Mexican soldiers attacked the Texas army at the Alamo. Sam then led the Texas army to victory at the Battle of San Jacinto. The leader of the Mexican army surrendered.

diorama of Mexican Army leader Santa Anna (standing at left) surrendering to a wounded Sam Houston

1829
becomes
Cherokee member

Time Line

1793
born

1808
runs away
from home

1814
fights in
U.S. Army

1823
elected to
Congress

Later Years

Sam was elected the first president of the Texas Republic in 1836. Texas became part of the United States in 1845. Sam was elected U.S. senator. He later was the governor of Texas.

Sam as a senator in 1854

1829
becomes
Cherokee member

1859
becomes
Texas' governor

Time Line

1793
born

1808
runs away
from home

1814
fights in
U.S. Army

1823
elected to
Congress

Sam Houston died in 1863. People remember that Sam helped American Indians. They remember that he helped Texas become a state.

1829
becomes
Cherokee member

1859
becomes
Texas' governor

1863
dies

Glossary

Alamo—a large building in San Antonio, Texas, where the Mexican army once defeated units of the Texas army; Sam Houston was not at the Battle of the Alamo.

American Indians—the people who originally lived in North America

Battle of San Jacinto—a battle in which Sam Houston led the Texas army to victory over the Mexican army; the victory gave Texas its independence from Mexico.

Cherokee—American Indians who once lived in the eastern United States; today Cherokee live mostly in North Carolina and Oklahoma.

governor—the leader of a state

lawyer—a person who is trained to give advice about the law

Mexico—the country that is south of the United States

Texas—a state in the southern part of the United States; the city of Houston, Texas, was named after Sam Houston.

Read More

Boraas, Tracey. *Sam Houston: Soldier and Statesman.* Let Freedom Ring. Mankato, Minn.: Bridgestone Books, 2003.

Woodward, Walter M. *Sam Houston: For Texas and the Union.* The Library of American Lives and Times. New York: PowerPlus Books, 2003.

Internet Sites

FactHound offers a safe, fun way to find Internet sites related to this book. All of the sites on FactHound have been researched by our staff.

Here's how:
1. Visit *www.facthound.com*
2. Type in this special code **0736823700** for age-appropriate sites. Or enter a search word related to this book for a more general search.
3. Click on the Fetch It button.

Index/Word List

Word Count: 248
Early-Intervention Level: 17

Editorial Credits

Mari C. Schuh, editor; Heather Kindseth, cover designer and illustrator; Enoch Peterson, production designer; Scott Thoms, photo researcher

Photo Credits

Corbis/Bettmann, 1
Library of Congress, cover, 4 (left)
North Wind Picture Archives, 12 (inset)
Photo Courtesy of Tennessee Historical Commission, 6
Sam Houston Memorial Museum, 4 (right), 10, 12, 18, 20; Dave White, 16
Stock Montage Inc., 8
The San Jacinto Museum of History, Houston, 14

Thank you to the staff of the Sam Houston Memorial Museum for providing the diorama image on page 16. The staff believes it is the first published image correctly showing Sam Houston with his left leg wounded. For more than a century, previously published images have incorrectly shown Houston with a wounded right leg.